For good cooks:
Alexis Krasilovsky,
Ann Beilis, Mildred Ross,
Alicia Seeger, Aura Herzog,
Haim Shapiro — P.K.

For Stephanie Calmenson — M.F.

A Parents Magazine
READ ALOUD AND EASY READING PROGRAM® original.

Distributed in Canada by Clarke, Irwin & Co., Ltd.
Toronto, Canada

THE MAN WHO COOKED FOR HIMSELF

by Phyllis Krasilovsky
pictures by Mamoru Funai

Parents Magazine Press ● New York

Library of Congress Cataloging in Publication Data
Krasilovsky, Phyllis.
The man who cooked for himself.
Summary: A man who lives at the edge of the
woods discovers that he need not rely on the
store for a supply of good things to eat.
[1. Food—Fiction] I. Funai, Mamoru, ill.
II. Title.
PZ7.k865Mal [E] 81-16904
ISBN 0-8193-1075-1 AACR2
ISBN 0-8193-1076-X (Lib. Bdg.)

There once was a man
who lived with his cat
in a little house on the edge of a wood.

He didn't have a wife or children
so he always cooked his own supper,
cleaned the house by himself,
and made his own bed.

The man didn't even have
a car or a telephone.
But he had a friend
who visited him every few days
bringing him the things he needed.

When summer came though,
the man's friend decided to take a trip.
So he told the man to order everything
he thought he would need for three weeks.

The man ordered meat, eggs, pretzels,
raisins, apples, lollipops,
crunchy peanut butter,

ketchup, carrots, onions, peppers,
pears, bananas, pickles —
and milk and sardines for his cat.

When he had put
everything away the next day,
the man decided
he would enjoy the summer
by doing nothing at all.
So he just sat in his
rocking chair in the sun.
And he grew lazier every day.
He grew so lazy, he did not even
want to cook for himself.

So, one day he made a big stew
that would last a long time.
He cut up carrots and onions,
peppers and meat,
and added salt and pepper.
He put everything into a big pot
and let it cook.

Then he sat outside enjoying the smell
of his stew cooking.

At night he went inside
and ate some of it.
It was delicious.
And it lasted for a whole week!

But a few days later,
he did not have much food left.
All he could find was salt, ketchup,
four peppermint sticks left from Christmas,
crunchy peanut butter, an overripe banana,
three pickles and an onion.
He mixed these things together in the pot
and went outside.

When the man tasted the stew that night
he did not think it was very good.
In fact, it was terrible.

"Ah, me," he said.
"I'm afraid I will just have to
go to sleep hungry."
Luckily, there was a little bit
of milk left over for the cat.

The next day the man
looked around the house
to see what he could eat.
His newspaper? No, that would give
him a stomach ache.
An old rag? A terrible idea!
Then he saw a fly whiz by.
No, he couldn't possibly eat that!

The man went out
to sit in his rocking chair
and enjoy the sun.
But all he could think of was food.

So he decided to go for a walk.
When he came to a stream,
he stopped to rest a while.
All of a sudden, he was
splashed with water.

At first he thought it had
started to rain.
Then he saw that fish were
jumping in the stream.
A fish had splashed him!
"Hmmm," the man said.
"Fish would be a good supper
for me and my cat."

Fortunately, he had some string
and a paper clip in his pocket.
He bent the clip into a hook
and tied the string to it.
Then he dug up some worms
to put on the hook.
In no time he caught four fish.

The man was very pleased with himself
and started home.
On the way, he looked down and
was amazed to find watercress
growing along the bank of the stream.
"So this is how it grows!" he cried.
He gathered a large bunch for salad
and put it in his hat.

When he bent down to pick up his fish,
he saw that there were
blue spots on his pants.
"That's funny," he said.
He looked around to see where
the spots had come from.

Right by his side was
a bush of blackberries.
He had rubbed against the berries!
The man saw birds eating the berries
so he knew they were good and tried some.
"They're delicious!" he cried.
"These are better than the ones
I buy in the store!"
And he put some in his hat.

Just then something hard plopped
on his bare head.
"What was that?" he asked.
He looked up and found
some apples growing on a tree.

"Apples! I love apples!" he said.
Soon his pockets were bursting with them.
The man began to look at things
more closely than he ever had before.

In front of him was a
giant oak tree full of acorns.
"Why, I can make pancakes out of them!"
the man said.
He shook the branches and
pounds and pounds of acorns
came tumbling down.

Then, since he couldn't carry anything else, the man went home.

He went to work right away
in his kitchen.

For dinner, he gave his cat
one of the fish.
The cat ate every bit of it,
then licked his paws and purred.
The man ate fried fish, watercress salad,
and berries for dessert.
He felt so good he almost
purred like his cat.

In the morning he ate
a delicious breakfast
of acorn pancakes and applesauce.

Then he went to sit outside
in his rocking chair,
as full and happy as he could be.
In the afternoon,
the man heard a car honking.
His friend had returned from his trip.

The man was proud of the delicious things
he had found to eat and
invited his friend to dinner.
Now when his friend asked him
what he needed, the man made sure to ask
for a book about gardens.
"Next spring I will plant
a vegetable garden,"
said the man.

All that winter the man
planned his garden.

His friend brought him
the seeds he wanted
and when spring came
the man planted them.

By summer, when the man's friend
left for his trip,
the man had tomatoes, green beans,
cucumbers, and corn
growing in his own garden.
He even had catnip for his cat.

And best of all, he was never so lazy
and he never went hungry again.

About the Author

PHYLLIS KRASILOVSKY thinks a little man
lives inside her somewhere. "He manages to
get out now and then through a book I write
about him," she explains. "I think it's fun
struggling with his problems, because he
always comes up with an ingenious solution."

Ms. Krasilovsky has written several
well-loved stories about THE MAN. This is
her first for Parents. She has also written
many other children's books, and articles for
newspapers and magazines in the U.S.,
Canada, England, and Israel.

Ms. Krasilovsky lives with her husband
and children in Chappaqua, N.Y. Her chief
pursuits besides writing are—gardening and
cooking, of course!

About the Artist

MAMORU FUNAI has illustrated many children's picture books. He loves illustrating books and, in his spare time, enjoys growing vegetables and flowers in his garden.

"I am always very happy with myself when a tomato ripens or a flower blooms. I especially like sharing my harvest with family and friends," says Mr. Funai. "So, I could well understand how happy THE MAN was to grow his own garden."

Mr. Funai was born in Hawaii, one of the most beautifully lush states in the country. He now lives with his wife and two sons in New Jersey—the Garden State, where else?

Parents Magazine Press is pleased to welcome both Phyllis Krasilovsky and Mamoru Funai to its group of authors and artists.

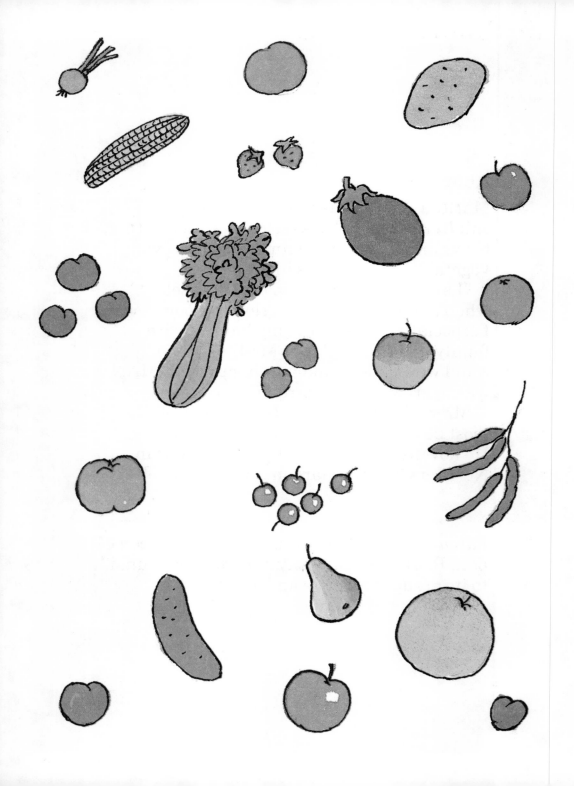